A Life to Share

Two Hundred Poems
for Living Life to the Fullest

John Schmidt

Path
Publishing

Amarillo, Texas

Path Publishing
4302 SW 51st #121
Amarillo, Texas 79109-6159
USA
www.pathpublishing.com
path@pathpublishing.com

Cover by Path Publishing and CreateSpace.com
Cover artwork supplied by Colourbox.com

To learn about John Schmidt, read About the Author at the end of the book. You can read about other books by John Schmidt or order copies—see Books and Ebooks by John Schmidt.

ISBN-13: 978-1-891774-81-2
ISBN-10: 1-891774-81-6

Printed in the United States of America

DEDICATION

For the spiritual seekers who continue despite
everything the world has to offer.

The Somewhat Misunderstood

People who sit on the sidelines, observing
others on the playing field and themselves,
are sometimes little understood by those
who are on the field.
Yet, someone must take the time
to discover the secrets of humanity
and the universe.

John Schmidt

ACKNOWLEDGMENTS

To my mother, who helped me put together my first book of poems, all written by other people, for a class assignment.

To Frances Clegg-Ferris, who for years has taught me about poetic forms, greatly enlarging the number of poetry types in this book.

CONTENTS

EXTENDED CONTENTS

Challenges 32

Older person experiences 41

Creative experiences 49

Spiritual experiences 80

INTRODUCTION

The first manuscript I submitted to a publisher, decades ago, was entitled *One.* It was a small collection of poems centered around personal development and the unity of humanity.

Through my years of writing, involving several genres—from nonfiction books to plays to poems to short stories—it is the poetry that has allowed me to best express myself. I truly feel that most people need to find some avenue of self-expression and self-revelation that allows a release of pent-up energies and also explores spiritual concepts.

I'm thankful that this craft of writing allows a person to not only go through self-transforming experiences, but also to create works of literature that have the potential of enabling other people to grow in unique and perhaps unforeseen ways. I hope you not only enjoy these poems, but also think about the ideas they express. As a person thinks, so he is—and will become.

The book is concerned with the concept of self-exploration by imagining the lives of other people. It is like a drama where the characters change frequently, while the theme of self-growth develops throughout the experience on stage. We are not creatures solely involved with physical existence, but spiritual beings who are going through a physical experience for the purpose of growing in ways we do not yet fully understand.

This is one reason why I write poetry, to

explore what I do not yet understand, and to better perceive the process we call life by delving into the ways words wind around ideas, ideas around spiritual concepts, and ultimately, spiritual concepts wind around our notions of God. Without examination into the existence of the Creator Who made everything, I see little reason to do or think anything.

A little about organization of this book: When a poem is not free verse, the poetic form is listed below. At the end of the book you will find a section that lists the definitions of forms used.

John Schmidt
June, 2017

Birth

"Basic Instructions For New People"

That was the sign across the wall.
So I joined the group and waited.
And waited.

And waited more.
Finally a man came and told us what to expect.
Disease, war, pestilence, unkindness—
with occasional love and patience thrown
in just for variety, but don't expect much.

When he was almost finished, a woman asked,
"Why does our Father send us into such a
place?"

Without much hesitation, as if he had heard
the question before: "It is not for me to explain
the procedure. The situation is for you to take
into yourself and find answers.
Will there be anything else?"

He went on to explain the process of
choosing parents and so forth.

We went along without further resistance.

Found Myself

Suddenly I found myself born.
To a mother who fed me with bottle
and was too busy to hold me in the night.
And to a father who added me to the
growing number of brats he had to feed.
Odd that my screams of terror
were interpreted as hunger.

Childhood experiences

Magnificent Mood

Sometimes I find myself in a silly mood.
I think even the cat objects.
Everything is funny. Nothing is *not* funny.
Everything is rosy. There are no problems.
No people upset me. All is seen in its best light,
everything everywhere at all times,
until the mood wears off.
I wish I could keep my silly mood for the rest
of my life, continuously silly. What a dream.

Remembering Life

Remembering life
events is less important
than first dreaming them

(Senryu)

Dog Understanding

Bad dog ran away when I called him,
snapped at the neighbor boy,
scared his little sister.
Refused to eat the dog meal I put out for him,
ate something dead out at the street instead,
upchucked the dead thing on the
living room floor,
 and was otherwise a bad dog.

But when he laid down by my bed at night,
 the look in his face was sorry, and I said
That's OK. You'll do better tomorrow.

Braided hair, freckles, and blue eyes

A six-mile walk with
you is easier than all
my walks after school

(Senryu)

The Ride Home

The Spin and Grin was a mountain of fear.
Lots of kids were all trying it, some of them
getting sick, one boy even laid down
on the rock way and got over it after a minute.
Three of them stupidly told the man
 to crank up the speed.
So he did. But he didn't tell the other people
that they were in for extra speed.
I think he enjoyed that, let out some of his
anger, as my dad would say.
I didn't go on the big ride that day.
I had to have time to think it over.
I rode on some of the other rides.
When my dad said it was time to go home,
I went with him and my brother and my
 sister without saying anything.
When I was in the back seat of car, I felt safe.

Childhood Objectives

To start
to understand what
one's life is all about, is the
essence of
childhood. To recall what Heaven
was like before coming here
is too.

(Cameo)

Two Weeks Later

It's a lonely feeling when your dog is gone.
It's a dog-gone bad time.

A week or two later Spider is still gone.
The ad Dad placed in the newspaper didn't work.
Spider can't read.
And if somebody picked him up, they don't
ever buy the newspaper.

If he does have a good home, I hope
he knows I miss him.
And I know I may never see him again until
 he and I get to Dog Heaven
 and can play again like we used to.

Boundless

A long white beard brought me to his lap.

I took up the boy and tried to get
a smile out of him.

As love, I stayed there for several minutes,
maintaining myself as two persons,
uniting a love of all grandchildren for
grandparents noticed for the first time.

Wish of Youth

Let me revel in my youthful days,
without any sorrow, in a way
I never before considered: a
chance to grow closer to
God so that throughout my life I may
find Him in all I do.

(Burns Stanza)

Bottom of the Eighth

When life
throws me a curve
I make it into a
fantastic curveball that strikes out
the side.

(Cinquain)

Young person experiences

Eighteen and Growing

Spend some time together with yourself,
getting to know who you really are.
You will be rewarded by not waking up
 50 years hence and wondering what happened.

(Epigram)

Wishing
is the essence
of productivity.
Without the first dream, all others
stay home.

(Cinquain)

Wonder
what you are when
you are young and you will
seldom wonder later where you
went wrong.

(Cinquain)

Nature looked me square
in the eye and told me, take
a hike—so I did.

(Haiku)

Hindfright

There was once a man named Jon
whose life purpose was to have fun.
When he died he discovered God's unction
had been left behind, totally undone.

(Clerihew)

Youthful Advice

Remember the words of your parents, my lad,
so your days will be long and not sad.
If you don't, your life may be a bother
'cause you'll find your wife much unlike your
    mother.

(Epigram)

Taming the Name Game

I tire of all this search for fame,
to garner this and that for the biggest Name.
If you want an example of a life without blame,
look to Jesus and live without shame.

(Epigram)

The Identity Question

"Will God
manifest Himself
at some point to humanity
or remain
a distant cousin?" He pondered
this thought as God waited in
his heart.

(Cameo)

School Planning

If you leave God out of education,
you generate mental mutilation.
If you make the Creator of the universe
    the core of education,
you create continual regeneration.
And a peaceful, prosperous nation
once the kids have assumed their positions.
Which would you prefer?

Looking Back, with No Great Admiration

Wisdom said I should seek first the
Kingdom of God but I,
in those sad days of youth, let "me"
be my god—so all I did seek
were ways of pleasure.

(Pento)

Wisdom Spoke Once

Wisdom stuck his head around the corner
and said, "Follow me."
But I said, "I've got to be free
and follow my friends' reality."
Wisdom did not persist or criticize me,
just let me continue my sure trip to the coroner.

(Epigram)

The Young Man Wanted to Know
Why He Was Born

The essence of life purpose
sometimes is most clearly
stated when a child among us
says, "I'm hungry," and with no fuss,
we make a sandwich.

(Pento)

Summer Fun, They Say

I wanted to climb the mountain until they laid
out the gear, gave me two jackets to wear,
explained the three day plan, told me about
folks last year who got lost and died—
hey, I had more fun in boot camp.
And I'm not even gettin' paid for this.
Wouldn't imagination work as well?

Purpose Proposed

The challenge has always been to find purpose
in the midst of everyday struggles, when there
seems to be no time for such flighty cares
of mind and soul. Yet taking time is a must.
Even the casual thinker has heard words such
as: The unexamined life is not worth bear-
ing. Let us then put aside our fears and dare
to be the people our Creator wants us
to be. When I was but a small child
I took time to think about things, in my
limited way. And perhaps I was more
in tune to purpose then, without the trials
adults seem so fond of. I had not yet died
to faith in a God Who I could love to live for.

(Italian Sonnet, with metric variety)

Reason to Live

Locating a reason to live
is not as hard as one
might suppose. Find something to give
to someone in need. Then, you deliv-
er love to your soul.

(Pento)

Truth Often Rides on the Back of Simplicity

Don't give up your chance
 to express yourself in a poem
in order to write a novel for
someone who is not listening.

(Epigram)

Piece together life
before I fall to pieces—
raise hands to Jesus

(Senryu)

Small bug—why do you
tempt me with size?—you know my
bigness means greatness

(Senryu)

Childhood anger has to be let free,
whether gotten over at 3,
23, or 103.

Common Sense Seeking

Seek wisdom first and not the wad
of money, allowing your days to be at peace.
If fortune gives you the nod,
so be it. Either way, your mind will be at ease.

(Epigram)

Go Go, Joe

All the crowds admired Fantastic Joe,
for about social events he was much in the
    know.
Yet about his spiritual, inner self
he could best be described as bereft.

(Clerihew)

A Little Advice Is All I Want

I sought the wisest man in the
world, or so the world said he be;
but he didn't have time to see me
because he was busy preparing for TV.

(Epigram)

Romance

Times Before

Let me
remember days
before I met you—but
wait, they are like shadows before
the light.

(Cinquain)

Passing Eyes

Her eyes met mine.
She was the girl for me.
But she was taller than me.
What would my parents think?

By the time that thought
passed through the matrix of my brain,
 she was gone down the subway.
I have never seen her again.

First love, the best love—
the one I will die with.
Not that any in between were of
 no consequence, just that the first kiss
was greatly appreciated
 by a teenager with little confidence.

The Romantic Dream

To be loved is the hope of us all,
to find one in the crowd that does fall
for our charms and our wit—
hopefully always sit
by our side, that first kiss do recall.

Dedicated to Helen and Richard Luecke
(Limerick)

Magnificent moon, why do you
seem so far away when you know
you are as close as her face?

The Z's Have It

Ziggy Zeporaus was always the last in his class
to be announced or called in the role;
this happened until college, when by chance,
Annie Zoot was the final name the professor
enunciated.
Ziggy literally turned around and stared at the
girl.
He caught himself—*She must think I'm a freak*—
and righted himself toward the front.
But after class he said to her in the hall,
"You must feel really down about being
always the last person to be called out."
"Not at all. My mom always told me,
they save the desert for the last."
He smiled, and never again felt that way
about being last to be named in all of his
other classes.

And Annie? She is proud to be Ms. Annie
Zeporaus, not even needing to
change the monogrammed
letters on her favorite jacket.

Marital Remiss

They never told me in Heaven
that I, in youth, needed
to be careful about who I married.
I thought it wisdom when
I wedded the first lass who would
kiss me.

(Cinquetun)

Great Thanks

When God began the universe I
think He had you in His mind. For why
else would He put all beauty in sky
and the earth in one face?
I thank Him for His goodness, to guide
me to my wife by grace.

(Burns Stanza)

Love Verse for the Happy Ones

"If you could love me as I love you,
I'd be as happy as bird in blue,
and almost as free." "You know I do,"
said she, all aglitter.
So they were married early in June—
ever glad he wed her.

(Burns Stanza)

Sweet Beth in Songwriting Class

The supposition in songwriting class
Was that a song could not have much
    substance.
I wrote this song to say I can love you
And not to common sense be all untrue.

My Love, I ask you not to look askance
At this semblance of lighthearted romance,
But keep me in your heart and all you do—
For I'll, in life and song, always be true.

(Song)

My Secret Place

Carry me Mabel into your
heart, for my love cannot
be measured as truest ardor
least it be held safe behind doors
that block worldly sight.

(Pento)

A Living Definition

Love is
defined in my old
dictionary as amorous
feelings. So
after forty years of wedded
bliss, what do you get, my friend?
Well, us.

(Cameo)

My Marvelous Lady

She was interested in me as a
soul, a human being.
I had not met anyone like her before,
at least not on a close basis.
So it took me some time to figure out.
In the meantime I fell in love with the girl.
We built a friendship, then a young marriage,
and three children for the world
 to deal with in their own time.

Once the children left home,
she was interested in me as a
soul, a human being.

Humor

Cat *Purrspective*

Silly cat, on porch, purring royally,
you think you are King of the
universe, when in reality
the only thing you own is me.

Dedicated to Animal Defence, a
Canadian organization devoted to
defending cats and other animals

The Wall's the Thing

Was Robert Frost whose poem spoke
that high fences made for
good neighbors. As for modern folks
in apartments, we mostly hope
for walls of concrete.

(Pento)

A Cloudy Issue

Bob: Did you hear about Fred? He was kicked
out of meteorological school.
Mona: Oh yeah? How come?
Bob: His teachers said he always had his head
in the clouds.

Moan Mona

Many articles, poems and songs have
mentioned Mona Lisa's subtle smile.
Someone, who shall remain anonymous,
suggested she was just hiding a set of bad teeth.

Bird Talk

I

Two women walk behind me.
Their banter is continuous.
But not as pretty as mockingbird in nearby tree.

II

Mockingbird's noise from sunup to sundown.
Imagine all the energy that uses.
No wonder birds die young.

III

Two mockingbirds carry on a conversation
on opposite sides of the street.
Probably a married couple.
I imagine what she is saying: "Kids are hungry.
Don't come home without worms."

Try This One on for Size

When I was small, I wanted to be big.
When I was an adult and big around the waist, I
 wanted to be small.
Funny how age is often irrelevant
and size, always an issue.

He thought he was a poet—
and that's good enough

I wondered if I could write a long poem—
say, four lines long. I gathered some
ideas, worked it out—busy as a bee.
The result? This poem about me!

Challenges

Give Me Some Time to Think About This

If God made me and Time, why is Time
always a nuisance, or a bother, or a concern?
When God made me on the Sixth Day,
on what Day did He make Time?

Maybe it was on the Eighth Day, an
afterthought.
Or maybe it was around before the whole
creative process started and He
couldn't get rid of it.

Or maybe Time is just our way of
associating physical happenings on
Earth and we shouldn't worry about it.

Whatever.

Another Awakening

So often do we forget the
reasons why we took life
on Earth until catastrophe
or long indolence shake us free
from a calm blindness.

(Pento)

Peace is
my companion
when I rest in God and
my goals and daily tasks abide
in Him.

(Cinquain)

The Clocks

They're always trying to stop us from being
Ourselves. Clocks, I mean. Those mentally
    attuned
Devices that have a face but no soul, that bring
Warning of other things not done and would
    soon
Have us stopping what we need most to be.
I smashed a clock once, as a boy, and was
Heartily scolded for the thing's death. I could see
Then it had no soul, but lost that sense because
As years went on they outnumbered my dreams.
Dreams are fragile—they have soul but only one
    face:
Mine. And I can only know them if I glean
Them from mirrored eyes that are not in a dead
    race
With clocks, who await me in every room of
My house, hungry little devils without love.

(Shakespearean Sonnet, with freedom of metric
forms)

Mild Determination

Within the walls of my heart are
dreams beyond my current
imagination, so why should I let
them stall because bizarre
circumstances come? I claim no
regrets.

(Cinquetun)

Progression Prescription

Remember the optimism at first
and the happiness coming at the end
and your middle will be easier.

Bring Him Home, My Captain

Through rough seas, around the Cape of Good
    Hope, I
Plead to you: Bring him home, my captain. Show
    him you
Are a man of courage when skies are blue
But there's no wind for days, or when the ship
    lies
Still in a fog's giant grip. If his friend dies,
Is draped under a flag, then let slide into
The sea, show patience in your eyes, and don't
    construe
That he is less of a man if he starts to cry.
Through port after port bring him home. And
    always give
Him good food, good water and company
While aboard. A late knock on your door,
    comfort
His soul if he should ask for that. So he can live
Free of debts, pay him at the end, and see
The smile you saw the day he came aboard.

(Italian Sonnet, with metric variety)

Smallest drop of rain
washes away all my tears
if desire is great

(Haiku)

Stress Mirror

Can we stop for a moment to examine
the nature of stress?
Is all stress bad?
When is stress bad?
How does stress affect the human body
and emotions?
Is stress first of all always a spiritual issue,
which trickles down to mind, emotions,
and body?

I heard these words from the lecturer and
I left the auditorium. If he was going to show
me myself, I had to get out of there.

Logic
tells me that adding
2 plus 2 equals 4. But when
I need to
add something plus infinity,
it fails. For those I rely
on God.

(Cameo)

So Which Will It Be?

They told him his name was Stevie Spence.
So he spent all his days in reverence
of a name, when in reality
he was a Spirit much closer to infinity.

(Clerihew)

Angels speak loudest
when we need silence the most.
Our job: to listen.

(Senryu)

The Least and the Greatest

The heights of our human understanding
are enlarged not just by the thinking
of our wisest, but by the wailing
of our saddest, whose needs
cause angels to gather around, bring
love to humanity.

(Burns Stanza)

First and First

Spirit
tries hard to find
the good in everything,
while the man sleeps on, seeks first his
TV.

(Cinquain)

Applause Is Not the First Cause

Robbie Robin was a singer of some notoriety—
how she could hit those high notes and bring
    harmony
to any audience. Yet in her nights after the
    shows
her inner, eternal sorrow only she did know.

(Clerihew)

Generational Regeneration

Mom said "You will be the death of me."
When she died three years later
I thought it was my fault.

Thirty years later I looked back on a sad woman.
When I almost made a similar statement to
one of my children, I caught myself.

We learn, not always quickly, but we learn.

Older person experiences

Life Joy

Life surprised me by giving me happiness.
 I was so shocked that I wanted most,
to continue.

Filtering the Divine Nature

Interesting how the biggest, most
Earth-changing idea needs
to be filtered through imagination
and the brain of a host
human who has courage to let
it come.

(Cinquetun)

Empire Poem

Can someone write a poem about a tall building?
Oh, I think so.
The craftsmanship in the wall decorations
and chairs in the foyer.
The strength of the steel in the unseen
structure.
The fact that it's still there after all these years,
all the winter storms, night's way
 below freezing, yet everyone toasty inside.
It has also survived New York City inflation,
where maintenance even on small issues costs
a fortune.
So I praise the men and women who designed it,
built it, and maintain it to this day.
When I look at it, I see not only its simple beauty
but its determination to survive in
an unhealthy world.

(Ekphrastic form)

Not Starving Anytime Soon

I watched those humanitarian shows on TV,
you know, where they show all the starving
children -- close-ups, never far away shots.
And I wonder if they are all starving.
I'm not saying that somebody is lying, or
that there aren't kids in Africa who need food.
I'm sure there are. But is it as bad as the
TV shows make it out to be?

Well, I turned down the volume and just
thought about it for a minute.
Even if they soak me for some money,
my heart is right about it.
So I wrote down their address.

Later that day I sent them $20.00 in the mail.
Maybe my $20.00 will feed a few kids for week.

Then I went into my kitchen and looked at
the cabinets full of food. It's going to be
a long time before I starve to death.
Maybe, in the end, my $20.00 is a thank you
note to God.

(Prose)

Food Truth

The food producers say GMO
is the way to go.
Go where? To the medical ward,
and then the grave, as we hoard
our Betsy Bits and cereals that
have in them, who knows what?
As their profits mount higher and higher
and we in our graves sink lower and lower,
when will we see that organic
is so much better than a trip on the Titanic?

The Why of Life with Strife

When I wondered why life
has so much strife,
I found no easy solution.
So I investigated evolution,
and found a long list of questions
with no good resolutions.

A friend led me to the Good Book,
and said that if I would only look
in there I would eventually see
that our world is not what was to be
when God designed the whole thing.
I saw that it was mankind who brings
so much chaos on their own heads.
So I blamed not God for this mess,
but set about by my own actions
to bring about an eternal resurrection
for us all.

The Day Another Change Came

The more I desire things to stay the same the
    more they change.
It's as if the planets in the solar system,
spinning as they do thousands of miles per
    hour,
insist that even the smallest creatures within
    their
great spheres conform.

Truth Sometimes Is Simply a Return

Let me hear most those dreams
before birth, where ideas were on rock-solid
universal principles and not
conformity to externals.

"How can I remember those?" you may ask.

By dreaming again tonight of life as a child,
then going one step further back.

Family Continuance

The wonders of life and Nature fill
me with admiration from this hill
overlooking crops and the old mill
that my great-grandfather
built by sweat. Sometimes I feel he still
comes home through the heather.

(Burns Stanza)

"I'm too busy for God."

Every
man seeks God in his
own way, was his philosophy.
Yet some may
be a lot slower than others.
He waited to his last breath
—too late?

(Cameo)

Pathways

Two paths crossed—
I took them both,
one in actual steps,
one in imagination.
One filled my senses,
the other my possibilities.
I really can't say which
was the most fun.

It Really Is

This is my lucky day. Though some say
this day is like others, in its way,
I say it is unique.
For on this day I seek
end to all that keeps my soul at bay.

(Limerick)

Creative experiences

Reader Query

1000 people may ask me to read
and define a poem, yet I cannot
if I did not live it,
and I cannot live it
if I have never visited the ambitions
within the 1000 people.

Not many haiku
 about wind only—few dreams
require mind only.

(Haiku)

Sometimes doing the very easy
with no stress is harder
than doing the very hard.

Diverse Words

I have no interest in writing a poem
until I have the freedom to write
poems about everybody.

One More Critic, Please

Critic: You say your book is about being
our ultimate, and yet it's full of silly humor
and the mundane. Why?

Author: We will never live our ultimate
unless we first live and understand
our simple.

Poems That Make Sense

Funny, how with all the changes
going on around me day after day
these poems go on.
They have solidified my steps,
give a sense to my walk.
Even though I may not know where
I'm going, in the ultimate destination,
 they make this part of the walk this day,
meaningful. And that says a lot.

Poem Philosophy

Properly speaking,
poem should speak
not just of property,
but propriety.

Timely Nature

If I ever complain about my workload,
in which I seldom get everything
done in one day, I need only look about,
to Mother Nature, who seems to get
everything done at her own pace.
And if she doesn't get something done,
she just puts it off until tomorrow,
and doesn't tell us.

The Creative Dilemma, Solved

I cannot—must not—will not be
rushed from creativity.
Deadlines, goals, ambitions—
 must not be allowed to stop me from doing
the beautiful—
for wherein can true satisfaction lie if not
in doing what is good, slowly, painstakingly,
 with details that will last the ages?

(Skeltonic)

Success is measured most
in the least amount of
distance between the man and
his God.

(Cinquain)

Project Source

You know it's from
God when the project
begins and ends
with relaxation.

Sad, But Ultimately True

There are some people who can't envision
wisdom in a poem simply because it is a poem.
English class in high school destroyed their
vision in memorizing Wordsworth at 11:00 p.m.

(Epigram)

Joy Upon Written Joy

They say lives are bound by ups and downs,
and I do not deny truth is found
in that. But my soul seems on sure ground
when I write verse day by
day so full of joy that astounds
all in me—sorrows fly.

(Burns Stanza)

The Maturing of Style

Wanted
to return to the
poems of my youth, where the words
flowed like
a river—that was sufficient.
Yet I could not. I needed
structure.

(Cameo)

The Gathering of My Friends

All my days are intertwined, surrounded
by these poems.
One could say they are my best friends.
Even before I was a child who was unable
to speak, I was practicing poems.
My last words on earth will most likely be a
poem—perhaps to an angel who happens by.

When I went off to college I had a going away
poem; when I graduated, a graduation poem,
though not exactly complimentary to the
education process, which was my trend
 in that day.

Now with more than 3000 of them I can
almost say that I'm satisfied, complete.

But then, there is this morning.

My Poems Are Shrinking, But
My Thoughts Are Going Higher

When I was a youth, I wanted to write
the poetic epic, one poem a whole book
or more, maybe a series.

In college I was happy to get an essay
knocked out with a passing grade.

Nowadays, a haiku will do,
if it touches someone.

Speak!

One
poem
requested
that I allow
it to speak for all
the poems I have written
in the last many years. I
wondered what it would say. Strangely,
it spoke mostly of questions not yet
answered by poems in the last many years.

(Etheree)

In all
the vicissitudes
of life this day comes down to one
poem. Not
so much successes in the world
but the process, unfolding
of me.

(Cameo)

Origami sheet
folded my soul to reveal
the edges of faith

(Senryu)

Oh Yes

It had been so long not writing a poem
that I forgot who I was.
They say that can't be done, but then,
most of them are not writers of poems.

Family experiences

The Burger Barrel

That burger is my burger.
I wish my older two brothers
wouldn't try to take my burger.
They think it's a game.
They have their own burgers.
Daddy bought a burger for all of us.
He loves all three of us the same,
like burgers.
We can all have on the burger what we want—
pickles, mustard, ketchup, maybe no lettuce.
That burger is my burger.

30 years later, my brothers on the West Coast
and not far from the West Coast, I
wonder if they are right now eating a burger.
Me having my own burger when I
was a kid was a matter of pride.
I wonder if Dad, now at that burger stand
in the sky, is adding ketchup.

Play Day

I seem to write serious poems.
My girl has not written a serious poem
in the first seven years of her life.
Hers are about games, dancing, the zoo (animals
are everywhere on her bedroom walls),
and people—some of whom I have met and
some not, some all in her imagination.

If only I could take a few ounces of her "play"
 into the deepest parts of my consciousness—
how then would my poems play out?
Would my life be different, looking back
on it in 50 years?

Times Change, But Often Stay the Same

Love
I had
never thought
about until
the day when she gave
me that look of interest
that went a little beyond
friendship but not to immoral
behavior. After six kids I think
I just got that same look, but no passion.

(Etheree)

No Fences Between Us

Let me recall life with you much more
than all the days that were mine before.
For life truly began when I tore
my shirt on the old fence
I was hired to mend. Was my core
feelings, you mended hence.

(Burns Stanza)

Thousand streams now
 one river—like my mother's love
infilling all my days.

(Haiku)

It's About Time, and Timelessness

One of the great things about following Jesus
 is that the fun doesn't stop at the
end of this world.
I mean, there will be other worlds,
other dimensions, other galaxies.

Who knows what we started when
my family and I sat down one day
 at the kitchen table and said we were
going to work together and
 make Jesus part of our family.

I have never regretted that, and I don't
 think any of the others have either.

Sometimes we just get bogged down
in daily stuff and don't see the eternity
in every moment, every decision,
every turn toward love.

Quiet Thoughts of Childhood

Let
me now
return to
a childhood of
love and attention,
where no matter mattered
more than me, or so it seemed.
Is this pride of which I speak? No,
just a statement of reality,
and of parental love lasting my life.

(Etheree)

What I Have Learned About Love

Love is
not a tragic thing
to be paraded on a stage
where he and
she suffer unrealized bliss—
but quiet strength to stand tall
through all.

(Cameo)

She Spreads a Big Table with
Her Small Hands

It has always amazed me how she
can make my day. We work hard, money
still a stranger to our place, but we
get by. I come in, rough
as the land, but her words soften me.
I think love *is* enough.

(Burns Stanza)

Time's Talent

Was I think, first her eye that caught mine,
then her face and sleek form. But was time
that made me bear her faults,
at first hidden—yet taught
me, in fifty years, love sublime.

(Limerick)

Wiser person experiences

The Heart of Time

Funny how you go from a year being 1/4
finished to 1/3 finished in only a month,
in the passing of April.
Then in two months you go to half the year gone.
Funny how you give birth to a child and
your youth is all gone, and when the child
graduates, adulthood is mostly gone.
And when you stand at the grave where you and
your spouse buried the child, the life
almost all gone.
Funny how in my imagination and my prayers
at night it's all alive and well.

Purpose
of life is to
create right results while
maintaining God space inside and
outside.

(Cinquain)

Peace Importance

Seems we all have issues every day.
Yet should we let them get in the way
of our peace? So what stands
of greater importance
than our walk with He Who wins each fray?

(Limerick)

See river not in
a hurry to get somewhere—
hurry would bring flood

(Haiku)

Happiness said to me,
"Why don't you just be still."
Finally, I am.

(Senryu)

The Observation Tower

I watched the ants for several minutes,
they not observing me at all,
intent on doing all that ants do before
 sundown and the cool the evening
shuts them down in their hole
and they relax, doing what ants
 do afterhours.

Only last week I was atop a skyscraper
in a large metropolitan area, which
shall remain nameless, and I observed
thousands of human beings down there,
 even smaller than the ants I observe today.
My mind noted great similarities, only
the people down there were certain
that their urges to produce were of far
greater value to the universe than the ants.

Confident Living

Within God, all of my needs are met.
When I look at years gone, was no debt
unpaid, no great desire
not financed. So I sire
no great fear of future things to fret.

(Limerick)

The Best Possible Partner

Wise is he
who gives God
the nod, allowing the
Creator of time and space
an important place
in his daily race.
By putting that Name
on his work he will find
himself far ahead in the game.

Winning Wisdom

Every time I visualize myself succeeding,
I see someone else losing.
This must go back to childhood.
I need to get away from this in all areas.

I need to see everything as a win-win.
God has enough for all of us.
In God's world, we can all win.
He sees us all as winners.

Final Words to an Audience
I Will Never See Again

I was at a conference.
I was given the chance to give the last word.
I was not an advertised speaker so I kept it
short.
Five minutes.

First, I gave thanks for all of them attending.
I summarized the main points of all the
speakers.

I told them that they could live their lives for the
next few weeks or months in two directions:

Ignore the advice and suggestions of the
speakers, and their lives would go on the same.

Put into practical application the main points of
the speakers, and perhaps even some smaller
points, and see changes that have ripple effects
that would benefit their family members, their
work environments, their communities, and
beyond.

The application of these new ideas might even
make its way into the deepest parts of their own
souls, leading to a whole new consciousness,
with a radical change by the end of the life—so
much so that there would be an internal
improvement in their spiritual selves, whereby in
times far beyond this lifetime their spirits would
see a greater affinity toward pure Love, the Love
that only God can express.

When I finished, there was some applause and there was silence at the same time. The applause, I appreciated. The silence I appreciated even more because I think it was caused by numerous individuals deeply considering what I had said.

(Prose)

Mortality for Morton Had Been Mostly Misunderstood

Morton Maxwell Smith discovered at the
     conclusion
of his life, he had been mentally clouded by
     evolution.
He did not find death and a grave completely,
was surprised by the face of God, an evaluation,
     and eternity.

(Clerihew)

About Time, Don't You Think?

I think it's time to take charge of life,
no more be content to follow the crowd,
to abstain from inner pricks, though they might
be from God. Time to take off my coward
suit and put on the full armor. Start a new way,
fully, here on my hundredth birthday.

(Epigram)

Not Ducking the Issue

Following along the country road,
I was stopped by a duck.
I knew it had seen me,
but it didn't seem agitated that
I had entered its space.
It went on contentedly picking
in the grass and the road.
I thought for a moment that it
was a tame duck, but that would
be unlikely. Though obviously it had
 been around people.
After I walked on by, I thought to myself,
"So should we be when facing all
new circumstances. Just keep
minding our own business and
letting things pass."

I'll Take It

Wisdom is to be sought like any
real thing—not like a commodity
on a shelf in a store,
imagination more
than truth—but as worthy as can be.

(Limerick)

An Odd Notion, When You Think About It

Silly to believe that God is stuck
on some remote corner of the universe
and gives no attention to us humans
here on Earth.
The only person who could believe such
an idea would be a very busy human,
trying to survive here on Earth.

Attitude for Success

Interesting how a person can
react to a challenge.
First is the fear reaction, that nothing
good can come of this, and
nothing does. With love, confidence
is king.

(Cinquetun)

Civilization Next

Wisdom
forces me to look
beyond circumstances into
a future
so bright that my fellow humans
must take a leap of faith to
see it.

(Cameo)

Unified Parts

Remember the wholeness in you
and you will receive a whole you.

Split apart the lives of other people
by unkindness and your wholeness
will be parted.

The infinity that you will one day long for
in eternity must be taken as a whole.

The Wisdom Walk

Wisdom met me halfway,
but only when I refused
the broad path of ignorance.

Height of It All

The height of a building is determined
not only by the distance from the ground
but also by its closeness to clouds.

Secrets Are Okay

The best place to hide Truth
is within something simple.
It will confound the most intelligent,
yet will yield to the most diligent.

Financial Sacrifices Sacrificed

When I want a life of luxury
I must think of the times when I'd be
hard at work and alone,
not with kin at my home.
So I think I'll just live modestly.

(Limerick)

Thanks for the Harvest

Sometimes we forget to say thank-you
to our friends, and they leave town,
most likely for forever, or we bury them,
with thank-you notes still growing
in the garden.

(Epigram)

Going Without, and Going With

Mother said to recall the
"lost children in Africa,"
so at church when the missionary came
I gave him my lunch money.
I found out later that day that he
was going to Indonesia, not Africa.
But I still went without lunch on Monday
and the hunger was the same.

Years later, a father of two children
who had never gone hungry one day,
perhaps not one meal,
I went to Indonesia.
My money then and years before,
was well spent.

(Prose)

Monuments and Memories

Make me a monument to one man's achievement
 and I will show you an item of bronze or clay.
Show me a monument to a life of service
 and I will show you a pair of old shoes
given the grandchildren after the funeral.

Water Relaxation

I relax best when nothing is drawing me
away from the feeling of nothing.

Like small waves caressing a beach,
none of them desires much attention.

Each simply states it is part of life;
that, for the time being, is enough.

Peace Positioned

Perfect
peace is not found
by striving, but in the
giving to God all that is not
 peaceful.

(Cinquain)

Trusting Unity

When I love my people all I can
I have touched, I believe, the right hand
of my God, Who made us
all alike. We should trust
in His design to unite our land.

(Limerick)

No Sorrow

Bring me no sorrow in the morning
for the dawn pronounces a new hope.

Bring me no sorrow at the noontime
for all the plants are a growin'.

Bring me no sorrow in the evening
for rest with my children is too complete.

Bring me no sorrow at the end of my days
for I lived each day to the best of my ability.

Bring me no sorrow in Heaven
for there is none there to be known.

Look

I wanted peace, so I left home for the city.
I wanted peace, so I left the city for places west.
I wanted peace, so I left those places for the
West Coast.
I thought about leaving the West Coast
for distant lands.
Standing on the beach looking out to the
Pacific Ocean, as I had once looked out over
the Atlantic Ocean, I decided, at last, that if
I really wanted peace, it had been in me
the whole time.

Spiritual experiences

Observational point of view about God

Man's problem is not that
God does not exist, nor that he thinks
God does not exist, but that he
does not fully believe that an infinite
God can coexist within an a finite
human being.
Thus he forever looks to external solutions
for what always has been an internal dilemma.

Let us pray for better.

Wise is he who does
not run from life, but let's God
run to him, in peace.

(Senryu)

Love Essence

Love is
the essence
of all things seen and the
primary energy in all
unseen.

(Cinquain)

Seeing Me Objectively

Let me see all the reasons why I
look so poor to the world and I'll find
mostly lies. But to look
on one page in God's book,
I'll see me described in the sublime.

(Limerick)

Success is every day
doing what God and I
most enjoy doing together.

Many Happy Returns

Someone asked me why I return
so often to my God when I churn
out verse. Perhaps it's because I learn
more about me when I
dwell on His goodness. Yea, my pur-
pose is found, by and by.

(Burns Stanza)

Illumination

She said, "Go out and greet the dawn."
Minutes later, pink sky
greeted the grass hill I was on,
the sun praising me for my long
fondness for beauty.

(Pento)

Wheel

The idea in all our circular ways
is to find the center of the circle,
which can only be done by coming out
of ourselves and allowing a secret Self
to be the hub on which we turn.

I cannot allow persecution
to slow my progress
towards resurrection.

The God Find

We need
to relax, even
in the search for God, which is not
as hard as
some people make it out to be.
For where could God be found but
in us?

(Cameo)

True Path

To love God is not wrong. In my heart
I know this to be true. When I start
to seek the confusion
which the world calls reason,
I must stop, return to love and art.

(Limerick)

By the Lake

Jesus
said, "Fear not my
little flock, for I have
overcome the world so you might
have life."

(Cinquain)

Nature, 1 million years.
Me, here 100 years, tops.
Nature, 1 million years.

(Haiku)

I emailed myself to God.
No attachments—nothing of this world.
Just, simply me.
I waited for a response.
It came: "I love you, too."

With Jesus, your...

Burden becomes your new beginning
Crisis becomes your thanks to Christ
Dilemma becomes your story of deliverance
Failure becomes your fantastic future
Frustrations become your freedom and
    satisfaction
Gross mistakes become your greatness
Heaviness becomes your hardiness
Mere sensations become marvelous miracles
Mediocrity becomes your meteoric rise
Mess becomes your message
Obstacle becomes your opportunity
Nuisance becomes your niceness
Pickiness becomes your patience
Problem becomes your praise
Quaking becomes your quietness
Sadness becomes your gladness
Test becomes your testimony
Trial becomes your triumph
Wrong headedness becomes your
    righteousness and your rightness

4:00 AM in the dark

Whisper
in my ear some
good news. "God loves you." I
know that, but it's nice to hear a
whisper.

(Cinquain)

Reading Love

The preacher said that we are no
longer under the old law, that grace
abounds, as does God's love.

With that being the case, I don't
have to write 1 million books in
order to someday get God's love.

I can just write this one for you,
it being an outflow of that love,
 and that will be sufficient, at
least for now.

Dedicated to Andrew Wommack

Turned Upwards

A life is touched on two points: birth and
transition.
The fulcrum on which life is elevated
is the "now" moment.
Let us continually reside in the love of
God so our thoughts and movements
bring harmony to the process that is
intent on elevating us, if we will allow it.

A *What If* Possibility

An older, wiser man than I once spoke...
"I leave you with this thought:
What if, by the simple declaration that
you are going to align yourself with
God in everything you do, you would
one day be as grand as one
of His universes?"

The Golden Penny

The little girl gave me her last penny.
Most likely the only penny she will
have this month.
I didn't know what to say, or do.

Rather than put it in the collection bag, I put
it in my pocket.

I don't think anyone saw me, and I don't
know what they would think if they did,
but it didn't matter. I wanted that penny.

30 years later, now back from the
missionary fields, I have that penny.
It's on the mantle next to the pictures of my
children and my grandmother and my wife.

For years, when I saw it, it would remind me
that when I have given everything,
give just a little bit more.

Dedicated to Pastor Joe Kirkwood
and others he has led on missionary trips

The Taking and the Giving

Years ago a man said to me,
"Nothing is ever lost in God."
Though he was talking about personal losses—
business, a wife, disappointments.

I wondered, "How does that work?"
I mean, we all have people who pass
 in and out of our lives, delays, maybe
 even tragedies.
So how does God restore us so that
those losses are not ends?

A few weeks later I was walking through a park
while going home and those ideas came
back to me, only it seemed like
answers were attached.

I saw a stream: a man rowing
and out of his boat items kept falling.
 But ever so often, things would float by
 that he would put in his boat.
But whatever happened, he and his rowing
and the stream continued on.

It is God's abundance, His love, that
continues, sustains, even increases
 beyond our present imagination, even
while some things are disappearing,
perhaps forever.

Peace Search

Peace is in finding
today what will be
most pleasing in eternity.

Angel Words

"Remember the spaces between the movements,
the silences between sentences in
the life you will live, for lying on those will
be the spiritual road you will travel."

I didn't quite understand what the angel said,
yet understood more when her words were
brought back to me about age ten,
as I lay in bed waiting for my friend sleep to
come again.

I think she meant to pay more attention to
my inner world in a world that is really
 stuck on itself.

Timeless river, I
see you most in my own soul—
we share same secrets

(Haiku)

Miracle upon Miracle

Something
of a miracle:
the day after a miracle,
there's a peace
in the home or motel room as
if nothing happened—we know
it did.

(Cameo)

The Small Will Make the All in Me

Let me
find my love of God
in the simplest of His wondrous
creations.
For in that I will find hallowed
communication and peace
with Him.

(Cameo)

All Thankfulness

When I thank God for the smallest
wonder that He put in me,
I better appreciate the *all-ness*
that only He can see.

Peace Is with Me Most

Peace
is with
me most when
I let it find
me. Not when I say
"On this day I will be
at peace throughout." But when I
simply leave the door open to
new adventures, overcoming all tasks
great and small. Then His peace is most
    revealed.

(Etheree)

Expanding Concern

To worship God is my purpose,
though there are some folks who
wonder why I'm concerned with "us"
far more than "I." It's a lacklus-
ter life if but me.

(Pento)

The Love Trip

Remembering to love others is
not as hard as we might suppose this
can be. Each of us has received kiss
from mother, a kind phrase
from stranger, a prayer from a sis-
ter or friend, Heaven's praise.

(Burns Stanza)

God's Work Now

Let me
go straight to God's work
for me, not need Him to tell me
ten times the
same message. So much time could be
saved and souls saved if we but
did this.

(Cameo)

A Very Spiritual Question

Jesus sincerely wanted to bring
us all under His care.
What could be so difficult in this?
Why have we taken on all the weight
of the world instead of running to
a smile and strong arms capable of
holding all at once?

Forgetting and Remembering

"I have not forgotten you, even though
you made your parents angry,
so angry that they kicked you out of the
house when you were 16 and
angry until you in a shower of tears
forgave them in a small church
in Tennessee.

"Remember me in your prayers,
for I was always praying for you,
 even before you knew how
 to spell the word."

Power of God not
just in stars and humans, but
smile in atom.

(Senryu)

Forgiveness Dream

Small image of two ladies, one brunette and one blonde, side by side like two photos, combined to make a single symbol repeated many times on a page.

The image was turned upside-down and repeated many more.

Then on an oversized page, right side up again, repeated many times until the images stop.

Intuitive knowing: the dreamer will repeat the process until she has forgiven self and others of everything.

Analysis the next morning: the brunette is the unforgiveness (dark thinking); the blonde is the proper image of self. These are in some kind of conflict because of unforgiveness toward self or someone in the outer world.

Question: What have I done in the recent past where I should have forgiven myself or someone else, yet have not. Though this could be a longstanding issue, covering months or years—maybe even decades.

Conclusion: I need to release all that, let it go, forget it. As it says in the Word, the Father has no remembrance of these things. Once I forgive everyone, He forgives me. Then I can forget the past and accept the new Christ future.

Transition

Which Is It?

Is a man to spend his life in pain?
Or is there much, much more to be gained
by attention to the way
of his God? Many a
man died but found his future, the same.

(Limerick)

Surprise, By in Large

Nobody told me I would never die.
So it was, by in large, a complete surprise.
If only someone had said a few words—
but then, perhaps they did, and I never heard.

(Epigram)

Time Has Its Limits

Time
started in
on me when
even a small
child, and has never
relented in its forced
march to a grave that means much
to it, yet nothing to me, a
risen Soul, united in the life
of God, Who first had the idea of Time.

(Etheree)

Fluidity

It's why older folks get rid of so much garbage.
That's why a man travels a thousand miles
to get forgiveness and say goodbye to a sister
he hasn't talked to in 30 years.
It's why dreams are sometimes so horrible,
almost nightmarish.

It's because everything that goes to Heaven
 has to squeeze through a tight funnel.
Garbage does not squeeze.

So I release her and everything about my life
that is in my mind and body and soul, energy
that is not fluid, is not like
the love of Jesus Christ.

It's that fluidity I'm trying to generate and allow
 to happen, so that when I go, there is no
garbage connecting me at all to what I once was,
to any old insistence on being selfish.

For I know that when I get to Heaven
there will be no remembrance of garbage.
There will be good memories of friends and
 family and society helping, but that's all.
 And that's all I need.

The Friendly Tombstone

Sometimes these words on the stones
make fun of those around,
But now that I'm here all alone,
I long most for the friends I never found.

(Epigram)

The magnet is attracted to...

"Location, location, location!"
announced the land magnet.
Funny, his latest development
seems so small here at his graveside.

At a Distance

Suddenly, quite unexpectedly, every obstacle
in the physical life vanished intently.
I stood on a hill and on all sides there
was nothing but air and distant vistas
that I imagined years ago but believed
could never exist anywhere.

You won't believe this perhaps, but an
angel was far distant in one direction.
I thought he would come to me, or I
go to him, but neither happened.

I remember now, he was assigned
to me as my guardian angel
through the entire physical experience,
and he was still with me.
What can I repay him for this service?
Nothing. Only God can.

What was it?

On the last day of my life I remembered
a promise I made to God
on the first.
It's the days between that seem so blurry.

I remember when...

Time
was when
I always
had plenty of
time—endless amounts
of it, or so it seemed.
Where did it go? Or was it
mostly in imagination
all the while? So its passing should be
no surprise, even to the newly dead.

(Etheree)

The Greeting

10,000 angels greeted me the day I died.
Too bad, back there,
I didn't know I had so many friends
in high places.

Too bad my survivors can't see us now.

At the Rewards Ceremony

I want to thank all who made this possible:
my mother, father, physical body,
all the angels who helped, the rough
people in the world who taught me lessons
(even though they didn't intend to).
And most of all, Brother Death,
who made me keep my attention to the plow—
 and even though I was a bit nervous,
went beyond.

Will it ever be too late to change the world?

I wanted to express love to a million people
but there wasn't time.

Funny how easy it is to desire
when they are all dead, or I am.

Remembrances

No one remembers the boy in shaggy pants
except the woman who gave him birth,
the man who buried him, and the
boy himself as a spirit in the next world.

Same

No matter how meteoric the rise to riches
    or fame
they always come home the same,
lying down, ready for rest in Heaven—
unless it's the other place because
they were always trying to get even.

(Epigram)

Separation Time

It's been a long time since I died.
They count it in years—what? Maybe 50?
I count it one eternity.

I am separated from them as a
great gulf separates two landmasses.
Yet I am separated from
God as if He was in the next universe
and I was on some remote moon in
 a dead solar system.

Simple wisdom
is more precious than
tons of gold;
just ask anyone who has died
with tons of gold but not
simple wisdom.

Eternity

Time Limitations

Eternity is a bold concept that
requires a long time to understand.

People who live only a short life,
yet wish to understand it,
must be willing to suspend disbelief.

No More Limits

Letting life live to the limit
is little more than luscious liquidity
of energy, not languishing on life's lacks
but localizing one's language into a ladder
to limitless love.

How long, Georgia?

It wasn't that I hated
Earth
  but that I had other places in the
  universe to go.
Was I to forever
maintain my stickiness
to a human body, brush my teeth
three times a day, go to the
  bathroom frequently, and miss
a reunion with stars?

(Skeltonic)

Heaven is not so much a place
but the ability, newfound,
to place yourself in space, any space,
by just a thought.
And that, is a wonderful thought.

Eternity Is Closer Than You Think

"Let me see God one more time before I die."
That was my thought, strange as it might
    appear.
For when I woke up from the physical life,
I found all light, and Him forever near.

Love
is that
beginning
where the motions
of the heart bring round
everything that a man
is, and makes smooth his rise in
elevated senses to a
space he never dreamed of, within the
presence of God, Who was and is that love.

(Etheree)

DEFINITIONS OF FORMS USED

Burns Stanza: six lines, with the rhyme scheme aaabab and syllable count of 999696

Cameo: seven lines unrhymed, in syllable pattern 2583872

Cinquain: five lines unrhymed, in syllable pattern 24682

Cinquetun: six-lines with the syllable count 8-6-10-6-8-2 and the rhyme scheme, axbaxb. Invented by E. Ernest Murrell.

Clerihew: a biographical poem, often humorous, with person's name in one line—two couplets

Epigram: a pithy poem, often with a twist at the end

Ekpstic form: about a work of art—painting, song, book, and so forth

Etheree: ten lines of increasing length, from one syllable to ten syllables in each line. No end rhymes. Etheree Taylor Armstrong was the originator.)

Haiku: Asian poem about Nature

Italian Sonnet: The idea is to establish a situation or a problem to be solved in the first eight lines and then give comments or a resolution in the final lines. Rhyme scheme is abbaabba cdecde, with variations in the last six lines. Also see Sonnet and Shakespearean Sonnet.

Limerick: consisting mostly of anapests, with a rhyme scheme of aabba—often humorous, but not always

Pento: five lines with the syllable count of 86885—the 8-syllable lines rhyme

Prose poem: consisting mostly of prose elements, much like those found in a letter, rather than a reliance on senses or flights of imagination

Senryu: Asian poem about humanity or things

Shakespearean Sonnet: Fourteen lines, iambic pentameter with the rhyme scheme, abab cdcd efef gg. The idea is to present three aspects of an issue with the final couplet giving some resolution. Popularized by William Shakespeare, it is also often called the English Sonnet. The author of this book prefers metric variety rather than a strictly iambic beat throughout. See Sonnet or Italian Sonnet.

Skeltonic, invented by John Skelton in 1460— multiple rhymes, tumbling helter-skelter. Short lines, sometimes rhymed four lines or three lines or two lines—sometimes no rhymes.

Sonnet: generally, a fourteen or fifteen line poem, iambic pentameter, focusing on a single theme or issue of a serious nature. Sonnets in this book may not be strictly iambic pentameter because the poet likes variety, in ideas and meter. See Italian Sonnet and Shakespearean Sonnet.

Song: often made up of four-line stanzas, with the rhyme schemes aabb, abab, or aaaa. Lines are similar in length, often close to iambic pentameter but not necessarily so. The lines need to be similar to each other in meter. A chorus can also be added, two lines or four lines, and it can be repeated.

ABOUT THE AUTHOR

John Schmidt has published almost two dozen works, through his publishing company, Path Publishing, six other publishers, and ebook publishers. For more than two decades he has been the editor of Path Publishing, releasing the works of more than twenty authors. In addition, he has earned Master's Degrees in English and in Drama; spent several years teaching college and high school English; penned more than 4,000 poems; developed skills for writing in several genres, from nonfiction books to plays to poems to short stories; and has always encompassed a great love for creative expression and the human experience. He lives in Amarillo, Texas, and is the Membership Coordinator for the Hi-Plains Poetry Society and Inspirational Writers Alive!, Amarillo Chapter.

Connect with John Schmidt

By e-mail: path@pathpublishing.com

Check out pathpublishing.com for more information about his books. On menu bar, click on "Most of the Books by John Schmidt" or "Personal Page for John."

Amazon.com Author Page: https://authorcentral.amazon.com/gp/ books/book-detail-page?ie=UTF8&bookASIN= 1500531316&index=default

Facebook John Schmidt:
www.facebook.com/john.schmidt.716195

Facebook Path Publishing:
www.facebook.com/pages/Path-
Publishing/110081005733297?sk=notes

LinkedIn: www.linkedin.com/in/path-
publishing-35097434/

Final words from John: "Many thanks to my
readers! Please remember to leave a review for
my book at your favorite retailer when possible."

Books and Ebooks by John Schmidt

Many of John's works can be ordered from
Amazon.com or by using PayPal at
pathpublishing.com. Most book descriptions are
at pathpublishing.com. On menu bar, click on
"Most of the Books by John Schmidt" or
"Personal Page for John."

You can also order paper editions or the audio
book by mail. The cost of the paperback edition
of *A Life to Share* is $7.99. Postage is $3.50 for
the first item and 75 cents for each additional.
With the shipping, the cost of one book is
$11.49. Texas residents need to add 8.25
percent sales tax which comes to $12.44. Send
bank check to Path Publishing, 4302 SW 51st
Ave. #121, Amarillo, Texas 79109-6159. For
inquiries, e-mail path@pathpublishing.com. Or
order a copy from Amazon.com. Thank you!

Other paperbacks for adults:

Timeless Sisters—A Novella About Love in All of Its Dimensions, $5.99. The cost of the Smashwords ebook edition of *Timeless Sisters* is $2.99 and can be ordered at Smashwords.com or its many apps.

Rock Solid Concrete Poems—Art Poems for the Heart, $7.99. Almost all of his art poems are in this paperback, at Amazon.com and pathpublishing.com. Here are short comments from a reviewer and three readers... "Poetry flows into shapes that pop off the page!" "Texas poet John Schmidt is a master at writing shaped verse/concrete poetry." "Well-crafted, humorous, and pleasurable—a sheer joy to ponder and to read aloud." "The poems are beautiful, not only in words but in design."

Winner's Wisdom—Eight-Week Devotional Using Poetry and Journaling to Express the Real You, $8.99.

My Return to the Future, 2350—Our Next Great Civilization Revealed, $9.99.

Forty Tips for Church Growth—A how-to guide for practical expansion, $4.99. Also an ebook for the same price at Smashwords.com.

Friends Forever, You and God—A Coloring Book for Adults and Children, $5.50.

My Visit to the Kingdom of God, $13.99.

Giving to Yourself and Letting Happiness Happen, $6.99.

Our Dream Language, $5.95.

Utopia II—An Investigation into the Kingdom of God, $3.50.

Audio book:

Silly Willy Will, a two-cassette collection of John's poetry, $6.00.

Paperbacks for youths:

The Lion Princess—Journey to an Awakening, $12.95.

Heroes, Angels and Miracles—Eleven Uplifting Stories from Around the World for Youths, $25.00, 360 pages. "Timeless Sisters" is one of the stories in this book.

Children's books:
Purchase all three for only $10.00.

Mr. Turtle's Award, $6.00.

You and God Together, Friends Forever, $6.00.

Two Stories for Children—Betty Blooper Is Super! and Hands Holding Heaven, bilingual, English and Spanish, $6.00.

His Smashwords ebooks:

Timeless Sisters, $2.99.

Forty Tips for Church Growth—A how-to guide for practical expansion, $4.99.

Lifetime collection CD:

If you enjoyed these poems by John, you can purchase more than 2,400 poems in *The Collected Works of John Schmidt (Third Edition),* a CD project in jewel case, which can be used on practically any computer. It includes almost everything he has written, excluding his most recent works: *My Return to the Future, 2350, Rock Solid Concrete Poems, Winner's Wisdom, Timeless Sisters,* and *A Life to Share.* It's like having many ebooks on your computer, at easy reach. The cost is only $15.99 at the pathpublishing.com shopping cart or by mail, plus shipping.

ABOUT THE PUBLISHER

Path Publishing began in 1993 and has published a variety of uplifting books and other projects over the years. The company tends to specialize in Christian nonfiction, poetry, biographies, and self-help. The website, pathpublishing.com, contains the works of numerous writers. In the past, the company has been in these publications: *Christian Writers' Market Guide, The Directory of Little Magazines and Small Presses,* and *The Writer.*

One final poem...

The Last Acceptance Speech

"I feel honored to accept this award tonight,
though it should go to the 1 million souls
who nurtured me through childhood,
protected me from foolishness in adolescence,
showed me the ways to go as a young adult,
gave me the courage to go through rough times,
led me to the good wife who cared for our
children, especially when I was traveling in
work, and led me to, eventually, an
understanding of Jesus that finished the life
that stands before you here today.

"I speak not only of people, but the invisible
angels who some people call the Holy Spirit.
In my wide experiences, I've come to the
realization that the Holy Spirit is, at least in
part, comprised of deceased human beings who

have come back from Heaven as astral entities or minds in order to help the foolish ones like myself, who never believed in unseen forces until near death.

"Again, I say thank you. And, once I pass through the transition and am reunited with my God because of their care (and the careful works of physical human beings who loved me, or at least tolerated me), may I never forget them. I will be forever grateful."

These were the words of a simple man who received accolades during his life, but never felt like he owned them. For he knew that without the help of the million, his work would have lacked force, intelligence, and peace.